Turn Your Passion
Into Profit:
How to Start
A Home-Based Business
And Achieve
Financial Freedom

I. Introduction

A. Explanation of the concept of turning passion into profit

B. Overview of the benefits of starting a home-based business

C. Importance of finding financial freedom through entrepreneurship

II. Finding Your Passion

A. Self-discovery techniques to identify your interests and skills

B. Understanding the market demand for your passion

C. Evaluating the potential profitability of your passion

III. Developing Your Business Plan

A. Understanding the key components of a successful business plan

B. Conducting market research and competitor analysis

C. Defining your target market and creating a marketing strategy

IV. Building Your Home-Based Business

A. Setting up a legal and financial framework for your business

B. Creating a professional image for your business

C. Utilizing technology and tools to streamline operations

V. Marketing and Sales

A. Developing a strong online presence through social media and search engine optimization

B. Building relationships with customers and networking with other entrepreneurs

C. Creating and implementing effective sales strategies

VI. Financial Management

A. Understanding the basics of financial management for a home-based business

B. Establishing a budget and keeping track of expenses
C. Generating and managing cash flow effectively

VII. Scaling Your Business

A. Identifying opportunities for growth and expansion

B. Building a team and delegating tasks effectively

C. Continuously monitoring and improving business performance

VIII. Conclusion

A. Recap of key takeaways from the book

B. Encouragement to take action and turn passion into profit

C. Final thoughts on achieving financial freedom through home-based entrepreneurship.

Introduction:

The world of entrepreneurship has evolved significantly in recent years, and starting a home-based business has become increasingly popular. With the advent of technology, it has become easier than ever to launch and run a business from the comfort of your own home. However, starting a business, regardless of its location, requires careful planning and hard work.

A. Explanation of the book's purpose and scope: The purpose of this book is to provide aspiring entrepreneurs with a roadmap to turn their passions into profit by starting a home-based business. This book is comprehensive in its scope, covering every aspect of starting and growing a successful home-based business, from assessing your skills and interests to creating a business plan, setting up your home office, building your business, and achieving financial freedom. Whether you're a seasoned entrepreneur or just starting out, this book provides the guidance you need to make your business dreams a reality.

B. The benefits of starting a home-based business: Starting a home-based business offers many benefits. For one, it allows you to be your own boss and work on your own terms. You have the flexibility to set your own schedule and work around your family and other commitments. Additionally, starting a home-based business can be much less expensive than starting a traditional brick-and-mortar business, and it allows you to reach a wider customer base through online platforms.

C. Importance of aligning passion with profit: One of the most critical elements of success when starting a business is finding a balance between your passions and profitability.

While it may be tempting to start a business solely for the purpose of making money, this approach is unlikely to result in sustained success.

On the other hand, starting a business based solely on your passions may not be economically viable. The key is to find a balance between what you're passionate about and what has a proven track record of success in the marketplace. By aligning your passions with profit, you will find more satisfaction in your work, and you will be more likely to achieve financial freedom.

Starting a home-based business is an exciting and fulfilling opportunity, but it requires careful planning and hard work. By following the guidance in this book, you will be well on your way to turning your passions into profit and achieving financial freedom.

I. Assessing Your Skills and Interests

Before starting any business, it is important to take a step back and assess your skills and interests. This self-reflection will help you determine if starting a home-based business is the right choice for you and will also provide valuable information for developing your business concept and plan.

A. Identifying your strengths and passions:

The first step in assessing your skills and interests is to identify your strengths and passions. What are you good at? What do you enjoy doing? Consider your hobbies, previous work experiences, and areas of expertise.

These skills and interests can provide valuable insights into potential business opportunities. For example, if you're passionate about cooking and have experience as a chef, starting a meal delivery service may be a great fit for you.

On the other hand, if you have a background in marketing and a passion for environmental issues, starting a sustainable product company may be a better match.

It's important to keep in mind that starting a home-based business doesn't require you to be an expert in a particular field. Instead, it's about identifying areas where you have skills and interests and finding ways to monetize them.

By aligning your passions with your skills, you'll find more satisfaction in your work and be more likely to succeed.

Taking the time to identify your strengths and passions is an important step in the process of starting a home-based business.

By doing so, you'll be better equipped to make informed decisions about the type of business you want to start and how to best utilize your skills and interests to achieve success.

B. Market Research to Determine Demand:

Once you have identified your strengths and passions, it's time to conduct market research to determine demand for your potential business idea. Market research is the process of gathering and analyzing information about your target market and industry to determine the viability of your business idea.

Market research is crucial because it helps you understand the needs and wants of your target market, identify your competitors, and determine the best way to position your business in the market. This information will also help you make informed decisions about your business concept, product or service offerings, and marketing strategy.

There are several methods you can use to conduct market research, including online research, surveys, and focus groups. When conducting online research, it's essential to review industry reports, analyze competitors' websites and social media accounts, and research relevant keywords to understand the demand for your product or service.

Surveys and focus groups can provide valuable insights into the attitudes and behaviors of your target market, and can help you identify any pain points that your business can solve.

It's also important to consider the competition in your industry when conducting market research. Look at the offerings of your competitors, and consider how you can differentiate your business to stand out in the market.

This could include offering a unique product, providing exceptional customer service, or utilizing innovative marketing strategies.

Market research is an essential step in the process of starting a home-based business.

> By conducting thorough market research, you'll be better equipped to make informed decisions about your business concept, target market, and marketing strategy, and increase your chances of success.

C. Identifying Gaps in the Market:

Once you have completed your market research, the next step is to identify any gaps in the market that your business can fill. A gap in the market refers to a need or demand for a product or service that is not currently being met by existing businesses. By identifying these gaps, you can create a unique business concept that will have a competitive advantage in the market.

> To identify gaps in the market, consider the following questions:
>
> 1. What pain points or challenges do your target customers face that are not being addressed by existing businesses?
> 2. What do your competitors offer, and how can you differentiate your business to stand out in the market?
> 3. Are there any new trends or technologies in your industry that you can incorporate into your business concept?

For example, if you are considering starting a home-based catering business, you may find that there is a gap in the market for healthy and sustainable food options.

You could differentiate your business by offering vegetarian and vegan options, using locally sourced and organic ingredients, and offering eco-friendly packaging.

Once you have identified gaps in the market, you can develop a unique business concept that will meet the needs of your target market and provide a competitive advantage in the market.

This will also help you differentiate your business from competitors and increase your chances of success.

Identifying gaps in the market is a crucial step in the process of starting a home-based business. By doing so, you'll be better equipped to develop a unique business concept that meets the needs of your target market, provides a competitive advantage, and increases your chances of success.

D. Determining if a Home-Based Business is the Right Fit for You:

Starting a home-based business can be an exciting and fulfilling opportunity, but it's not right for everyone. Before taking the leap, it's important to determine if a home-based business is the right fit for you.

There are several factors to consider when deciding if a home-based business is the right choice, including:

1. Work-Life Balance: One of the benefits of a home-based business is the flexibility to create a better work-life balance, but this also means that it can be challenging to separate work and personal life. Consider if you have the discipline to maintain a healthy balance between work and personal life.

2. Time and Financial Commitment: Starting a business requires a significant time and financial commitment. Make sure you have the time and resources to devote to starting and running a successful business.

3. Entrepreneurial Mindset: Being an entrepreneur requires a certain mindset, including a willingness to take risks, resilience, and the ability to adapt to change. Consider if you have the personality traits and skills needed to be successful as a home-based business owner.

4. Support System: Running a home-based business can be lonely and isolating at times. Consider if you have a strong support system, including family and friends who can provide encouragement and support during the ups and downs of starting and running a business.

5. Home Environment: Starting a home-based business requires a dedicated workspace, which can be challenging if you have limited space or distractions at home. Consider if you have a suitable environment to work from home and maintain productivity.

Starting a home-based business can be a fulfilling and rewarding experience, but it's essential to determine if it's the right fit for you before taking the leap.

Consider the factors listed above, and be honest with yourself about your strengths, limitations, and goals. By doing so, you'll be better equipped to make an informed decision about whether a home-based business is the right choice for you.

III. Creating a Business Plan

A. Developing a Business Concept:
A business plan is a roadmap for the success of your business, and it all starts with a clear and well-defined business concept.

A business concept is a brief statement that describes what your business does, who it serves, and what makes it unique.

When developing a business concept, consider the following steps:

1. Refine your product or service: Based on your market research and assessment of your skills and interests, refine the product or service you will offer. Be specific about what you will offer, who you will serve, and what makes it unique.

2. Define your target market: Identify the specific group of customers you want to serve. Consider factors such as age, gender, location, income, and interests. This will help you better understand the needs and wants of your target market and tailor your product or service to meet their needs.

3. Identify your unique value proposition: What makes your product or service unique and different from your competitors? What problem does it solve for your target market, and how will it meet their needs better than any other business? Your unique value proposition should be the foundation of your business concept.

4. Articulate your mission and vision: Your mission statement should clearly communicate the purpose of your business and what it aims to achieve. Your vision statement should articulate your long-term aspirations for your business and what it will look like in the future.

By developing a clear and well-defined business concept, you'll have a better understanding of what your business does, who it serves, and what makes it unique. This will also provide a foundation for creating a comprehensive business plan and help you stay focused on your goals as you start and grow your business.

Developing a business concept is an essential step in creating a business plan and starting a successful home-based business.

By taking the time to refine your product or service, define your target market, identify your unique value proposition, and articulate your mission and vision, you'll be better equipped to achieve your goals and achieve financial freedom through your home-based business.

B. Defining Your Target Market:

Defining your target market is one of the most important steps in starting a successful home-based business.

Your target market is the specific group of customers you want to serve and sell to. By understanding the needs and wants of your target market, you can better tailor your product or service to meet their needs and increase the chances of success for your business.

To define your target market, consider the following steps:

1. Identify demographic information: Demographic information includes factors such as age, gender, income, education, location, and family status. This information can help you understand the basic characteristics of your target market and better tailor your product or service to meet their needs.

2. Understand their interests and needs: Conduct market research to understand the interests and needs of your target market. This can include conducting surveys, focus groups, or analyzing data from social media and other sources. This information can help you better understand what motivates your target market and what they are looking for in a product or service.

3. Identify your ideal customer: Once you have a better understanding of your target market, identify your ideal customer. This is the person who is most likely to buy your product or service and is the most important target for your business. Consider factors such as their income, location, interests, and purchasing behavior to better understand your ideal customer.

4. Segment your market: Based on your research, you may find that your target market can be further divided into smaller segments, each with their own unique needs and wants. By segmenting your market, you can better tailor your product or service to meet the specific needs of each segment and increase the chances of success for your business.

Defining your target market is an important step in starting a successful home-based business. By taking the time to understand the needs and wants of your target market, you'll be better equipped to tailor your product or service to meet their needs and increase the chances of success for your business.

By segmenting your market and identifying your ideal customer, you'll be able to focus your efforts and resources on the most important targets for your business and achieve financial freedom through your home-based business.

Creating a Financial Plan

A. Estimating startup costs

B. Projecting income and expenses

C. Seeking funding options

D. Implementing a bookkeeping system

A. Estimating Startup Costs:

Before starting your home-based business, it's essential to estimate your startup costs. This will help you determine how much money you'll need to get your business up and running, and will also help you create a realistic financial plan.

Consider all expenses related to starting your business, such as equipment and supplies, marketing and advertising, and any necessary licenses and permits.

Make sure to also factor in any costs related to operating your business from home, such as utilities and rent.

B. Projecting Income and Expenses:

Once you've estimated your startup costs, you'll want to create a financial plan that projects your income and expenses.

This will help you understand how much money you'll need to cover your expenses and start generating a profit.

Consider creating a budget that breaks down your monthly expenses, including both fixed and variable expenses, and projecting your monthly income based on your target market and sales projections.

C. Seeking Funding Options:

If you need additional funds to start your home-based business, there are a variety of funding options available.

This can include personal savings, loans from friends and family, and loans from banks or other financial institutions.

You may also consider crowdfunding or seeking investment from angel investors.

Be sure to research the different funding options and consider the terms and conditions of each option before making a decision.

D. Implementing a Bookkeeping System:

To ensure the success of your home-based business, it's important to implement a bookkeeping system that tracks your income and expenses.

This will help you make informed decisions about your business, and will also make it easier to file your taxes.

Consider using a simple bookkeeping software or hiring a bookkeeper to help you manage your finances.

Creating a financial plan is an essential step in starting a successful home-based business.

By estimating your startup costs, projecting your income and expenses, seeking funding options, and implementing a bookkeeping system, you'll be better equipped to achieve financial stability and long-term success.

Setting Goals and Objectives

A. Defining your vision

B. Setting SMART goals

C. Creating an action plan

D. Measuring progress and making adjustments

A. Defining Your Vision:

Before setting your goals and objectives, it's important to define your vision for your home-based business.

What do you hope to achieve through your business, both in the short-term and the long-term?

This vision will serve as a guiding light as you set your goals and create your action plan.

B. Setting SMART Goals:

Once you have a clear vision for your business, it's time to set specific, measurable, achievable, relevant, and time-bound (SMART) goals.

This will help you stay focused and motivated as you work towards your vision.

Consider setting goals in areas such as sales, customer acquisition, and product development, and make sure each goal is aligned with your vision for your business.

C. Creating an Action Plan:

With your goals in place, it's time to create an action plan that outlines the steps you'll take to achieve them. Consider breaking down each goal into smaller, manageable tasks, and assign a timeline for each task. This will help you stay on track and keep your focus on what's most important.

D. Measuring Progress and Making Adjustments:

Once you have a plan in place, it's important to regularly measure your progress and make adjustments as needed.

This will help you ensure that you're on track to achieve your goals and make any necessary changes to keep your business moving in the right direction.

Consider using tools such as progress reports, customer feedback, and data analysis to measure your progress and make informed decisions about your business.

Setting goals and objectives is a critical step in the success of your home-based business.

By defining your vision, setting SMART goals, creating an action plan, and regularly measuring your progress, you'll be better equipped to achieve your desired outcomes and grow your business over time.

V. Outlining Your Marketing Strategy

A. Understanding your target market

B. Selecting the right marketing channels

C. Creating a budget

D. Measuring the effectiveness of your marketing efforts

A. Understanding Your Target Market:

Before you can develop an effective marketing strategy, it's important to understand your target market.

Who are your ideal customers and what do they need or want from your business? Conducting market research and customer surveys can help you gain a deeper understanding of your target market and tailor your marketing efforts to meet their needs.

B. Selecting the Right Marketing Channels:

Once you understand your target market, it's time to select the right marketing channels to reach them. This could include social media, email marketing, content marketing, or paid advertising. Consider your target audience, your budget, and your goals when selecting the right marketing channels for your business.

C. Creating a Budget:

Marketing your business can be expensive, so it's important to create a budget that you can realisticallystick to.

Consider both the upfront costs of each marketing channel and the ongoing costs, such as the time you'll need to spend creating and distributing content. Be realistic about your budget and make adjustments as needed to ensure you're able to achieve your marketing goals.

D. Measuring the Effectiveness of Your Marketing Efforts:

Once you have a marketing plan in place, it's important to regularly measure the effectiveness of your marketing efforts. This will help you understand what's working well and what needs improvement.

Consider using tools such as analytics and customer feedback to measure the success of your marketing efforts and make adjustments as needed.

Developing a marketing strategy is an essential part of growing your home-based business.

By understanding your target market, selecting the right marketing channels, creating a budget, and measuring the effectiveness of your marketing efforts, you'll be better equipped to reach your target audience and achieve your business goals.

IV. Setting Up Your Home Office

A. Determining the Ideal Workspace

B. Creating a comfortable and productive work environment

C. Organizing your work area

D. Ensuring adequate storage and space

A. Determining the Ideal Workspace:

When setting up a home office, it's important to determine the ideal workspace that will meet your needs.

Consider factors such as natural light, privacy, and access to power and internet. It's also important to choose a space that's separate from your living space, so you can focus on work and avoid distractions.

B. Creating a Comfortable and Productive Work Environment:

Creating a comfortable and productive work environment is key to staying focused and motivated while working from home.

This could include investing in ergonomic furniture, decorating your workspace with plants or artwork, and choosing colors that create a positive and inspiring atmosphere.

C. Organizing Your Work Area:

Keeping your work area organized is essential for staying productive and reducing stress.

This could include using desk organizers, filing cabinets, or a whiteboard to help keep your workspace clutter-free.

D. Ensuring Adequate Storage and Space:

Adequate storage and space is critical for a home office, as it allows you to keep your workspace organized and prevents clutter.

Consider investing in storage solutions such as bookshelves or file cabinets, or using a spare room as a dedicated office space.

Setting up a home office is an important step in starting a home-based business.

By determining the ideal workspace, creating a comfortable and productive work environment, organizing your work area, and ensuring adequate storage and space, you'll be better equipped to work effectively and achieve your business goals.

B. Purchasing Equipment and Supplies

Starting a home-based business requires investing in equipment and supplies that will help you run your business efficiently and effectively. Here are a few key items you may need to purchase:

1. **Computer and Printer:**

    A computer and printer are essential tools for most home-based businesses. Consider investing in a high-quality computer that is fast, reliable, and has enough memory and storage to meet your needs. Additionally, a printer with scanning and copying capabilities can be useful for a variety of tasks.

2. **Office Furniture:**

    Investing in ergonomic office furniture such as a desk, chair, and lamp can help you create a comfortable and productive work environment.

3. Consider your specific needs and choose furniture that is adjustable, supportive, and will help you maintain good posture.

4. **Software and Tools:**

   Depending on your business, you may need to purchase software and tools such as accounting software, project management software, or graphic design software. Research your options and choose tools that are best suited to your business needs.

5. **Communication and Networking Devices:** Devices such as a telephone, internet router, and Wi-Fi router can help you stay connected and communicate effectively with customers, suppliers, and employees.

6. **Stationery and Supplies:**

   Basic office supplies such as paper, pens, and folders are necessary for most businesses. Consider ordering custom stationery and business cards to help build your brand and make a professional impression.

When purchasing equipment and supplies, it's important to consider quality and durability, as well as price.

While it can be tempting to purchase the cheapest items available, investing in quality equipment and supplies can help your business run more smoothly and save you money in the long run.

Purchasing the right equipment and supplies is crucial for starting and running a successful home-based business.

Consider your specific needs, research your options, and invest in quality items that will help you run your business efficiently and effectively.

C. Ensuring Legal Compliance

Starting a home-based business requires ensuring that you are in compliance with all relevant laws and regulations. Here are a few key areas to consider when it comes to legal compliance:

1. **Zoning Laws:**

    Before starting a home-based business, it's important to research and understand the zoning laws in your area. In many cases, you may need to obtain a special permit or license to operate a business from your home.

2. **Business Licenses and Permits:**

    Depending on your business type, you may need to obtain a business license or permit to operate legally. Check with your local government for specific requirements in your area.

3. **Taxes:**

    Home-based businesses are subject to the same tax laws and regulations as any other business. Ensure that you are aware of the tax implications of starting and running a home-based business and plan accordingly.

4. **Insurance:**

    Insurance is an important part of protecting your home-based business. Consider obtaining liability insurance to protect against potential lawsuits and property insurance to protect your equipment and supplies.

5. **Trademarks and Intellectual Property:**

    If you are using a specific name or logo for your business, consider registering it as a trademark to protect your brand.

Additionally, ensure that you are not infringing on anyone else's intellectual property rights by using logos, images, or other materials without permission.

Ensuring legal compliance is a critical part of starting and running a successful home-based business.

Take the time to research and understand the laws and regulations that apply to your business, and consult with a lawyer or accountant if you need additional guidance.

By doing so, you can ensure that your business is legally compliant and that you are protected against potential liabilities.

D. Creating a Budget for Startup Costs

Starting a home-based business can be a cost-effective way to become your own boss, but it still requires an investment of time, effort, and money.

To ensure that you have the resources you need to get your business off the ground, it's important to create a budget for your startup costs.

Start by making a list of all the costs you will incur in the early stages of your business. This might include expenses such as:

1. Equipment and supplies: This can include things like a computer, printer, office supplies, and any other tools or materials you need to run your business.
2. Legal and professional fees: This can include costs associated with obtaining a business license or permit, registering your business, and seeking legal or accounting advice.
3. Marketing and advertising: To get your business off the ground, you may need to invest in marketing and advertising to reach your target market.

4. Rent or mortgage payments: If you're using your home as your office, you'll need to factor in the cost of rent or mortgage payments into your budget.
5. Insurance: As mentioned earlier, insurance is an important consideration when starting a home-based business. Ensure that you budget for insurance costs, including liability insurance and property insurance.
6. Miscellaneous expenses: There may be other miscellaneous expenses associated with starting a home-based business, such as internet and phone costs, utilities, and supplies.

Once you have a complete list of your startup costs, prioritize the expenses based on importance and allocate your resources accordingly.

It's also a good idea to build a cushion into your budget to account for unexpected expenses.

By creating a realistic budget, you can ensure that you have the resources you need to get your home-based business off the ground and on the path to success.

V. Building Your Business

A. Establishing an Online Presence

In today's digital age, having an online presence is essential for any business, including home-based businesses. Establishing an online presence can help you reach a wider audience, increase your visibility, and establish your brand.

Here are a few steps to help you get started:

1. **Choose a domain name and website platform:** Select a domain name that reflects your brand and is easy to remember.

    Consider using a website builder platform such as WordPress or Wix to create a professional-looking website without the need for technical skills.

2. **Develop a website:** Your website should be clean, visually appealing, and easy to navigate.

    Make sure it includes all the important information about your business, such as products or services offered, contact information, and business hours.

3. **Start a blog:** Blogging can be a great way to engage with your audience, share your expertise, and drive traffic to your website. Choose a blog platform and start publishing relevant, informative content on a regular basis.

4. **Utilize social media:** Social media platforms such as Facebook, Instagram, and Twitter can be valuable tools for reaching your target market and building relationships with customers. Decide which platforms are best for your business and create a strategy for engaging with your followers.

5. **Consider e-commerce:** If you plan to sell products or services online, consider setting up an e-commerce platform to streamline the process. Popular options include Shopify, BigCommerce, and Magento.

By establishing a strong online presence, you can reach a larger audience, build your brand, and ultimately, drive sales for your home-based business.

Just remember to keep your website and social media channels up to date and engaging to ensure that your customers continue to find value in your online presence.

B. Networking with Other Businesses

Networking is a crucial aspect of building any business, including home-based businesses. By networking with other businesses, you can form partnerships, find new customers, and gain valuable insights into your industry.

Here are a few ways to start networking:

1. **Attend local events**: Attend local events and conferences related to your industry. This is a great opportunity to meet other business owners, exchange ideas, and potentially form new partnerships.

2. **Join business organizations**: Consider joining business organizations, such as chambers of commerce or industry-specific groups. These organizations often host events and provide opportunities for members to network and collaborate.

3. **Participate in online communities:** Join online communities, such as LinkedIn groups, that are relevant to your industry. This can be a great way to connect with other business owners, exchange ideas, and find new customers.

4. **Host events:** Hosting events, such as workshops or meet-ups, can be a great way to network with other businesses and showcase your expertise. This can help establish your brand and attract new customers.

5. **Collaborate with other businesses:** Consider collaborating with other businesses to cross-promote each other's products or services. This can help expand your reach and bring in new customers.

By networking with other businesses, you can gain valuable insights into your industry, form partnerships, and find new customers.

Just be sure to approach networking with an open mind, be respectful of others, and be willing to offer help as well as receive it.

C. Finding and Reaching Customers

Finding and reaching customers is a critical step in building a successful home-based business. Without customers, you won't have a business. Here are some tips to help you find and reach your target market:

1. **Know your target market:** Before you can reach customers, you need to know who they are. Define your target market by considering factors such as age, location, income, and interests.

   This will help you create a marketing plan that is tailored to their needs and preferences.

2. **Use social media:** Social media is a powerful tool for reaching customers.

   Choose the platforms that are most relevant to your target market and use them to engage with potential customers, share content, and promote your products or services.

3. **Utilize SEO:** Search engine optimization (SEO) is the process of optimizing your website to rank higher in search engine results pages (SERPs). This can help you reach more customers and increase your visibility online.

4. **Leverage content marketing:** Content marketing is the process of creating and sharing valuable, relevant, and consistent content to attract and retain a clearly-defined target market. This can include blog posts, videos, e-books, and more.

5. **Offer promotions:** Consider offering promotions, such as discounts or special offers, to attract new customers. This can help you build a customer base and generate buzz about your business.

6. **Partner with other businesses:** Consider partnering with other businesses to reach new customers. For example, you could offer to cross-promote each other's products or services.

By finding and reaching your target market, you can increase your customer base and grow your business.

Be creative, be persistent, and be willing to experiment to find what works best for your business.

D. Managing Your Finances

Managing your finances is a critical aspect of running a successful home-based business. Here are some tips to help you manage your finances effectively:

1. **Create a budget:** A budget is a financial plan that outlines your expected income and expenses. By creating a budget, you can track your spending and ensure that your business is financially viable.

2. **Keep track of your expenses**: Keeping track of your expenses is crucial for managing your finances. Make sure to keep receipts, invoices, and other records of your spending. This will help you accurately track your expenses and ensure that you are on track with your budget.

3. **Use financial software:** Financial software can help you manage your finances more efficiently. Consider using a program like QuickBooks or Xero to track your income and expenses, generate financial reports, and manage your accounts payable and receivable.

4. **Separate personal and business finances:** It's important to keep your personal and business finances separate to avoid confusion and ensure accurate financial reporting. Consider opening a separate business bank account and using a separate credit card for business expenses.

5. **Monitor cash flow:** Cash flow is the amount of money that is coming in and going out of your business. Monitoring your cash flow will help you stay on top of your finances and avoid financial difficulties.

6. **Seek professional advice:** If you are unsure about how to manage your finances, consider seeking professional advice from an accountant or financial advisor. They can help you create a financial plan and provide guidance on managing your finances effectively.

By managing your finances effectively, you can ensure the financial stability of your business and achieve your financial goals.

Regularly review your finances, seek professional advice if needed, and be prepared to make adjustments as needed.

E. Building a support system

Building a support system is crucial for the success of any home-based business. As a sole proprietor, it can be easy to feel isolated and overwhelmed by the various responsibilities of running a business.

A strong support system can help provide you with the encouragement, motivation, and resources you need to succeed.

There are several key components to building a support system:

1. Finding a mentor: A mentor can provide you with guidance, advice, and support as you navigate the challenges of starting and growing your business. Look for someone who has experience in your industry or has started their own successful business.

2. Joining a business network or community: Being part of a group of like-minded individuals can help you stay motivated and connected. There are many local and online groups specifically for home-based business owners that you can join.

3. Working with a virtual assistant: If you find yourself drowning in administrative tasks, consider hiring a virtual assistant to help you manage your schedule, handle emails, and take care of other day-to-day tasks.

4. Building a team: As your business grows, you may want to consider hiring additional employees or contractors to help you manage the workload. Building a team can help you delegate tasks, freeing up time for you to focus on growing your business.

Having a strong support system in place can make all the difference when it comes to successfully running a home-based business. By seeking out help and resources, you'll be better equipped to overcome challenges and achieve your goals.

VI. Growing Your Business

A. Expanding your customer base

Growing your business is an exciting and crucial stage in the development of your home-based enterprise. In this section, we will discuss various strategies for expanding your customer base and taking your business to the next level.

A. Expanding Your Customer Base: One of the most effective ways to grow your business is by expanding your customer base. This involves reaching new customers through marketing and networking efforts, as well as by offering new products and services. Some strategies for expanding your customer base include:

1. **Marketing campaigns:** Utilize various marketing channels such as social media, email marketing, and search engine optimization to reach new customers and promote your products or services.

2. **Networking:** Networking is an essential component of business growth. Attend trade shows, participate in industry events, and join business organizations to meet potential customers and build relationships.

3. **Diversifying your offerings:** Offer new products or services that complement your existing offerings, or explore new market segments to expand your customer base.

4. **Utilizing customer referrals**: Encourage satisfied customers to refer their friends, family, and colleagues to your business. Offer incentives for referrals, such as discounts or rewards, to incentivize your customers to spread the word about your business.

Expanding your customer base is crucial for the growth and success of your home-based business. By utilizing these strategies, you can reach new customers and grow your business to new heights.

B. Diversifying your product or service offerings

As your business grows and gains traction, it is important to consider expanding your product or service offerings. This not only helps you reach new customers, but also provides additional sources of revenue and helps to insulate your business against any potential downturns. There are a few strategies you can use to diversify your offerings.

1. **Offer complementary products or services.** Consider what other products or services your customers might need that complement what you already offer. For example, if you sell handmade jewelry, you might also offer custom gift wrapping or a line of jewelry storage products.

2. **Enter new markets.** Consider expanding into new markets that are related to your existing business. For example, if you run a home-based bakery, you might consider branching out into catering or offering meal delivery services.

3. **Develop new products or services.** Look for opportunities to innovate and create new products or services that meet the needs of your customers. This could involve using your existing skills and knowledge in new ways, or exploring new areas of expertise.

4. **Consider licensing or franchising.** If you have a successful business model, you might consider licensing or franchising your business to others. This can help you reach new markets and increase your brand recognition, while also providing additional revenue streams.

When diversifying your offerings, it's important to do your research and make sure that there is demand for your new products or services.

You should also assess the costs and resources required to launch and maintain these new offerings, and make sure that they align with your overall business goals and objectives.

C. Hiring employees

As a home-based business owner, you may find that as your business grows, you need additional help in order to keep up with the demand.

Hiring employees can help you take your business to the next level and achieve even greater success. However, it's important to approach this step carefully, as it can also bring a whole new set of challenges.

Before hiring employees, consider the following:

1. **Determine the need:** Consider whether hiring employees is necessary for your business. Can the work be outsourced or managed through contractors? Will it help you grow your business or is it simply a way to ease the burden on yourself?

2. **Legal compliance:** Make sure you understand and comply with all local, state, and federal laws regarding hiring employees. This includes obtaining necessary licenses, paying taxes, and following labor laws.

3. **Budget:** Determine how much you can afford to pay employees and set a budget accordingly. You'll also need to factor in additional expenses such as benefits, insurance, and equipment.

4. **Job description:** Create a detailed job description that outlines the responsibilities, duties, and expectations for the position. This will help you attract the right candidates and set clear expectations from the beginning.

5. **Recruitment:** Choose a method for finding and attracting candidates. This may include online job postings, word of mouth, or local classified ads.

6. **Interviewing:** Develop a process for interviewing and evaluating candidates. This should include an assessment of their skills, experience, and personality.

7. **Training:** Plan for how you will train your new employees. This may include on-the-job training, workshops, or online courses.

By approaching the process of hiring employees with careful consideration and planning, you'll be able to build a strong team and take your business to new heights.

D. Delegating Tasks to Free Up Time

As your business grows, it's important to have systems in place to help manage the increasing workload.

Delegating tasks to employees or contractors is an effective way to free up your time and focus on the core aspects of your business.

However, it's important to delegate tasks wisely to ensure that the quality of your work is maintained. Here are some tips for delegating tasks effectively:

1. **Identify tasks that can be delegated:** Take a look at your daily tasks and identify which ones can be performed by someone else. Consider tasks that are repetitive, time-consuming, or do not require your expertise.

2. **Choose the right person for the job:** Consider the skills and experience of your employees or contractors when delegating tasks. It's important to match the task with the right person to ensure that it is completed to the desired standard.

3. **Provide clear instructions:** When delegating tasks, be sure to provide clear instructions on what needs to be done, by when, and how it should be done. This will help ensure that the task is completed correctly and efficiently.

4. **Set expectations:** Be clear about your expectations for the task and any deadlines that need to be met. This will help keep everyone on track and ensure that the task is completed on time.

5. **Provide support:** Provide support and guidance to the person you are delegating the task to. This may include training, access to resources, and regular check-ins to ensure that they have everything they need to complete the task effectively.

By delegating tasks effectively, you can free up your time and focus on growing your business. This, in turn, will help you achieve financial freedom and reach your long-term goals.

E. Continuously improving and updating your business plan

As your business grows, it is important to continually reassess and adjust your plan to stay ahead of the competition and meet the changing needs of your customers.

Delegating tasks, expanding your customer base, diversifying your offerings, and hiring employees are all important steps in growing your business, but it is also important to take a step back and evaluate the overall effectiveness of your plan.

To continue the success of your home-based business, it is crucial to make regular updates to your business plan.

This includes taking into account the latest market trends, customer feedback, and changes in your personal and professional life.

Your business plan should be a living document that evolves as your business grows. It should outline your goals, strategies, and action steps, and serve as a roadmap for your business.

As you reach each goal, it is important to assess your progress and adjust your plan accordingly. This includes revisiting your target market, updating your marketing strategy, and reassessing your finances.

In addition to regularly reviewing and updating your business plan, it is important to stay informed about the latest developments in your industry.

This includes attending trade shows and networking events, reading industry publications, and participating in professional organizations.

By continually improving and updating your business plan, you can stay ahead of the competition and achieve long-term success for your home-based business.

VII. Achieving Financial Freedom

A. Staying on top of finances and cash flow

In order to achieve financial freedom as a home-based business owner, it's crucial to stay on top of your finances and cash flow.

This means having a clear understanding of your income and expenses, and consistently monitoring both to ensure that your business is profitable.

One of the benefits of starting a home-based business is having more control over your finances. However, this also means having more responsibility to keep track of your financial situation and make decisions that will positively impact your bottom line.

Some steps you can take to stay on top of your finances and cash flow include:

1. Maintaining accurate and up-to-date financial records, including invoices, receipts, and bank statements.
2. Creating and adhering to a budget that aligns with your financial goals and objectives.
3. Keeping track of your expenses and analyzing your spending to identify areas where you can reduce costs.
4. Regularly monitoring your cash flow to ensure that you have enough funds to cover your expenses and keep your business running smoothly.
5. Seeking the advice of a financial professional, such as an accountant or financial advisor, if needed.

By taking these steps, you can build a strong foundation for financial stability and set yourself on a path towards achieving financial freedom as a home-based business owner.

B. Creating multiple streams of income

Creating multiple streams of income is a crucial step towards achieving financial freedom.

This means that instead of relying on a single source of income, you will have several sources of income that complement each other and help you maintain a steady flow of income.

There are various ways to create multiple streams of income, including:

1. Offering additional services or products related to your core business: If you already have a home-based business, you can expand your offerings to increase your income. This can be as simple as offering a new service or product that complements what you already offer.

2. Starting a side hustle: A side hustle is a secondary business that you run alongside your main business. This can be anything from freelance writing to pet sitting to tutoring.

3. Investing in stocks, real estate, or other ventures: You can invest in stocks, real estate, or other ventures to earn passive income. This income is generated from investments that do not require much effort from you.

4. Renting out a room in your home: If you have extra space in your home, you can rent it out for additional income. This is a simple and low-risk way to earn extra money.

Creating multiple streams of income can help you achieve financial freedom by providing a safety net in case one stream of income dries up.

It also helps you increase your overall income, which can lead to more financial stability and security.

Creating multiple streams of income is a crucial step in achieving financial freedom.

This means diversifying your sources of income so that you have a more stable financial situation. In other words, having a variety of income sources can help you minimize the impact of a potential income loss.

For example, if you have a home-based business that generates your primary source of income, you could supplement that income by offering freelance services or renting out a room in your home.

Alternatively, you could invest in stocks, bonds, or real estate to generate passive income.

When considering creating multiple streams of income, it is important to evaluate each opportunity carefully.

You should only invest in sources of income that align with your skills and interests, and that offer a positive return on investment.

Additionally, you should consider the amount of time and effort required to generate each stream of income, as well as any associated risks.

Creating multiple streams of income is about spreading your financial risk and increasing your financial stability.

It requires careful planning, research, and execution, but it can pay off in the long run by providing you with greater financial freedom.

C. Building a savings and investment plan

Building a solid savings and investment plan is crucial for achieving financial freedom, especially for business owners.

It not only helps you prepare for emergencies and unexpected expenses, but it also gives you the financial stability to make long-term investments that can help grow your business.

Here are a few steps to help you build a savings and investment plan:

1. **Establish an emergency fund:** This fund should be used to cover unexpected expenses such as medical bills or car repairs, or to cover your personal and business expenses during a temporary income loss. Aim to save at least 3 to 6 months' worth of living expenses.

2. **Prioritize debt repayment:** If you have high-interest debt, such as credit card debt or personal loans, prioritize paying it off first. High-interest debt can be a hindrance to achieving financial freedom and can negatively impact your credit score.

3. **Diversify your investment portfolio:** Consider investing in a mix of stocks, bonds, and other assets to help reduce your overall risk. Consult a financial advisor to determine the best investment mix for your specific financial goals.

4. **Start a retirement plan:** A retirement plan, such as a 401(k) or individual retirement account (IRA), can help you save for the future and take advantage of tax benefits.

5. **Automate your savings:** Make it easier to save by setting up automatic transfers from your checking account to your savings account or investment account.

By following these steps, you can build a strong savings and investment plan that will help you achieve financial freedom.

Remember, it's never too early or too late to start planning for your financial future.

D. Minimizing debt

Debt can be a major burden on your financial stability and limit your ability to achieve financial freedom.

As a home-based business owner, it's important to minimize your debt as much as possible.

There are several strategies you can employ to help reduce your debt and improve your financial situation.

1. **Make a budget:** Creating a budget is a crucial step in managing your finances and reducing debt. By tracking your income and expenses, you can identify areas where you can cut back and redirect that money toward paying off debt.

2. **Prioritize your debt:** Take stock of your debts and prioritize them based on their interest rate and the amount owed. Consider paying off high-interest debts first, as they will cost you more in the long run.

3. **Negotiate with creditors:** If you're struggling to make payments, reach out to your creditors and see if they can offer any help, such as a lower interest rate or a payment plan.

4. **Avoid taking on new debt:** While paying off debt, it's important to avoid taking on new debt. This means avoiding using credit cards and avoiding taking out loans unless it's absolutely necessary.

5. **Consider a debt management plan:** If you're struggling to manage your debt on your own, consider seeking the help of a debt management company. They can negotiate with creditors on your behalf and help you create a payment plan that works for you.

6. **Increase your income:** Increasing your income can help you pay off debt faster. Consider taking on a side hustle, selling products or services, or finding ways to increase your business's revenue.

Minimizing debt is an important part of achieving financial freedom as a home-based business owner.

By creating a budget, prioritizing your debt, and finding ways to increase your income, you can take control of your finances and work toward your financial goals.

E. Balancing work and personal life

Balancing work and personal life is essential for achieving financial freedom and overall well-being.

When starting a home-based business, it can be challenging to separate work from personal life, as the line between the two is often blurred.

However, finding a balance is crucial to avoid burnout and maintain a healthy lifestyle.

Here are a few tips to help you balance work and personal life:

1. **Set boundaries:** Decide on specific work hours and stick to them, just as you would with a traditional 9-5 job. Make sure to also set aside time for personal activities, such as exercise, hobbies, and spending time with loved ones.

2. **Create a designated workspace:** Having a dedicated workspace can help you stay focused and mentally separate work from personal life. When you're finished with work, close the door to your office or leave your workspace to signal the end of the workday.

3. **Take breaks:** Regular breaks help you recharge and avoid burnout. Take short breaks throughout the day to stretch, take a walk, or simply relax and recharge.

4. **Prioritize self-care:** Taking care of yourself is crucial for maintaining a healthy work-life balance. Incorporate activities such as exercise, mindfulness, and self-care into your routine.

5. **Learn to say no:** It's important to set limits on the amount of work you're willing to take on. Saying no to additional work or projects will help you avoid overloading yourself and maintain a healthy work-life balance.

By implementing these tips, you can maintain a healthy balance between work and personal life.

Remember, achieving financial freedom is not just about making money, but also about having the time and energy to enjoy the fruits of your labor.

VIII. Conclusion

A. Recap of key points

In conclusion, starting a home-based business is a thrilling journey that requires careful planning, hard work, and dedication.

To help ensure your success, it's essential to follow a structured process that covers all the key aspects of starting a business.

The eight stages outlined in this guide, from identifying a gap in the market to achieving financial freedom, provide a roadmap to help guide you on your journey.

A. Recap of key points:

- Identifying a gap in the market and determining if a home-based business is the right fit for you
- Creating a comprehensive business plan that includes defining your target market, creating a financial plan, setting goals and objectives, and outlining your marketing strategy
- Setting up your home office, including determining the ideal workspace, purchasing equipment and supplies, ensuring legal compliance, and creating a budget for start-up costs
- Building your business by establishing an online presence, networking with other businesses, finding and reaching customers, managing your finances, and building a support system
- Growing your business by expanding your customer base, diversifying your product or service offerings, hiring employees, delegating tasks to free up time, and continuously improving and updating your business plan
- Achieving financial freedom by staying on top of finances and cash flow, creating multiple streams of income, building a savings and investment plan, minimizing debt, and balancing work and personal life

B. Final Thoughts and Encouragement

Starting a business from the comfort of your home is an exciting journey.

It takes passion, dedication, hard work and persistence.

However, it is important to remember that success does not come overnight. Building a successful home-based business takes time and effort, but the rewards can be significant.

With the right approach and mindset, you can turn your passion into profit.

Encouragement is essential when starting a business. It is easy to get discouraged by obstacles, setbacks and failures along the way.

However, it is important to keep a positive outlook and maintain a growth mindset. Believe in yourself and your ability to succeed, and never give up on your dreams.

Surround yourself with supportive people who believe in you, and seek guidance from experts in your industry.

Starting a home-based business is a challenging but rewarding journey. With the right planning, strategy and effort, you can turn your passion into a profitable venture.

The key to success is to stay focused, stay motivated, and continue learning and growing as a business owner.

Remember, success is not a destination, but a continuous journey of growth and improvement. With the right mindset, you can achieve financial freedom and turn your passion into profit.

C. Next steps for turning passion into profit

Starting a business takes effort, dedication, and patience. However, with a well-thought-out plan and a clear understanding of your goals and objectives, you can turn your passion into a profitable venture.

The key is to stay focused, keep learning, and be open to new ideas and opportunities. Here are some next steps you can take to help ensure your success:

1. **Implement your business plan:** Your business plan is your roadmap to success. Use it to guide your decisions and actions as you start and grow your business. Remember, your plan is a living document that should be updated regularly as your business evolves.

2. **Stay organized:** Make sure you have systems in place to keep track of your finances, customer information, and sales. A well-organized system will help you stay on top of your business and make better decisions.

3. **Monitor your progress:** Regularly review your financial statements and compare them to your projections. This will give you insight into how your business is performing and help you make necessary changes to stay on track.

4. **Seek feedback:** Ask your customers, employees, and others in your network for their opinions on your business. Listen to their feedback and use it to make improvements.

5. **Keep learning:** Stay up to date on industry trends, best practices, and new technologies. Read books, attend workshops and conferences, and connect with other business owners.

D. Acknowledgments and resources for further learning and support

Starting a business can be challenging, but it doesn't have to be done alone.

There are many resources available to help you on your journey, including local business organizations, online forums, and business incubators.

Here are some additional resources to help you succeed:

1. **Small Business Administration (SBA):** The SBA offers a range of resources, including counseling, training, and funding, to help small businesses start and grow.

2. **SCORE:** SCORE is a nonprofit organization that offers free business mentoring and workshops to help entrepreneurs succeed.

3. **Local Chamber of Commerce:** Your local Chamber of Commerce can provide you with networking opportunities, access to business resources, and information on local business events.
4. **Online forums:** Join online forums to connect with other business owners and entrepreneurs. These forums can be a great source of support, advice, and inspiration.
5. **Business incubators:** Business incubators provide workspace, mentorship, and resources to help new businesses grow and succeed.

In conclusion, starting a business can be a challenging but rewarding experience.

With a solid business plan, a clear understanding of your target market, and a supportive network, you can turn your passion into a profitable venture.

Remember to stay focused, stay organized, seek feedback, and keep learning.

Good luck on your journey!

www.ingramcontent.com/pod-product-compliance
Lightning Source LLC
Chambersburg PA
CBHW071124240526
45465CB00023B/829